POCKET IMAGES

Balham & Tooting

The Duchess Palace theatre, Balham Hill, *c.* 1906.

POCKET IMAGES

Balham & Tooting

Patrick Loobey
& John W. Brown

NONSUCH

PATRICK LOOBEY was born in 1947 and has lived in Balham, Putney, Southfields and Streatham—all within the Borough of Wandsworth. He joined Wandsworth Historical Society (founded 1953) in 1969 and has served on its archaeological, publishing and management committees, being chairman of the society from 1991 to 1994. Having collected Edwardian postcards of Wandsworth borough and the surrounding district for nineteen years, he has a wide-ranging collection, encompassing many local roads and subjects.

Patrick privately published a volume of postcard views of Putney and Roehampton in 1988 and another on Battersea in 1990. Forthcoming titles will include Streatham, Wandsworth, Putney and several other areas.

Reproductions of all the views in this book are available from Patrick Loobey, 231 Mitcham Lane, Streatham, London, SW16 6PY (081 769 0072).

The captions to the photographs in this book are but a brief glimpse into the varied and complex history of the area. For those seeking further information, the Wandsworth Historical Society covers the borough's boundaries, publishing a journal and various papers, the fruits of members' research. Monthly meetings are held on the last Friday of each month at 8 p.m. at the Friends' Meeting House, Wandsworth High Street.

The author must thank and recommend the Local Library at Lavender Hill, Battersea, where early newspapers, deeds and directories, maps and parish records are made available to those wishing to research names, dates and addresses of families or business concerns.

JOHN W. BROWN has lived in Streatham all his life. His family has a long association with the area dating back to the 1880s, when his great grandfather, John Brown, moved to what was then a semi-rural country town on the outskirts of London.

His interest in local history was aroused when researching his family tree, in response to pleas for help from relatives in America, who were keen to learn about their roots in the UK. His fascination with the subject was encouraged by his father, Leslie Brown, who, when recalling his childhood adventures in the area at the time of the First World War, spoke of a locality which bore little resemblance to the Streatham of today.

John has written a number of books on the history of Streatham and the surrounding area and also publishes reprints of classic histories of the region written in the eighteenth and nineteenth centuries. He is a member of the Local History Group of the Streatham Society and the Southwark and Lambeth Archaeological Society and regularly gives talks on the history of Streatham.

First published 1994
This new pocket edition 2007
Images unchanged from first edition

Nonsuch Publishing Limited
Cirencester Road, Chalford
Stroud, Gloucestershire, GL6 8PE
www.nonsuch-publishing.com

Nonsuch Publishing is an imprint of NPI Media Group

British Library Cataloguing in Publication Data.
A catalogue record for this book is available from the British Library.

ISBN 978-1-84588-468-0

Typesetting and origination by NPI Media Group
Printed in Great Britain

Contents

Central Hall, Mitcham Road, *c.* 1914.

Nightingale Lane in winter, 1909.

Introduction

The story that unfolds through the medium of the photographs in this book concerns the expansion of two small villages during the 63-year reign of Queen Victoria and beyond into the twentieth century.

Tooting was first mentioned in a Saxon charter dated AD 675; and in the eleventh century the de Gravenel family owned the manor, hence the full, now defunct, name Tooting Graveney.

Following the Norman invasion of 1066 the Abbey of Bec in Normandy was awarded the manor of Upper Tooting, which it kept until 1370. The name Tooting may refer to a 'toot', or look-out post, which was probably erected at the end of the Roman period as part of a protective screen around London against Saxon raids. Tooting High Street and Balham High Road are both on the alignment of the Roman Stane (stone) Street from London to Chichester. Tooting was still rural up to the First World War; walking near the open fields of the Furzedown area it was not unusual to smell new mown hay.

Balham, probably no more than a farmstead during the Saxon period, was originally called Balgenham. The Abbey of Bec owned some land in the area, but it was not until 1542 that the more modern name of Balams appears as the name of the farm. The eighteenth century saw the appearance of various farms and by the 1850s country mansions were built along the high road for city merchants. The late Victorian period, however, saw parcels of land sold off for commercial development to house the incoming merchants, semi-professionals and artisans wishing to move into the expanding suburban town.

Balham has been the 'gateway' to the south for almost 1,900 years, many years before Peter Sellers used that line in a radio spoof on Balham in the 1960s.

The Wheatsheaf public house, Upper Tooting Road, *c.* 1918.

One

Mitcham Road

Tooting Junction tram terminus, c. 1913. The London County Council (LCC) extended the tram service as far as Tooting Junction on 13 October 1907. The South Metropolitan Electric Tramway from Croydon was supplied with power from overhead cables, while the LCC trams were powered via a conduit in the road. The terminus was a very busy spot as passengers changed trams to continue their journey. Note the newly erected pillar box on the right, bearing King Edward VII's initials.

Tooting Junction railway station, *c.* 1914. The first station at Tooting was opened on 1 October 1868 and was closed for passenger traffic soon after the present station by the bridge was opened in Mitcham Road in 1894. The tracks on the right were the Merton Abbey line which is no longer in operation.

The Tooting locomotive, *c.* 1910. The London, Brighton and South Coast Railway named a number of their D-class suburban locomotives after local towns. At times this led to confusion as those not familiar with the idea thought the names indicated the destination of the trains! (See also p. 73.)

Mitcham Road in around 1912 showing the parade of shops and houses between Renmuir Street and Otterburn Street. A delivery boy can be seen standing next to his bike outside No. 276, the butcher's shop of J.C. Coppin—'Purveyors of high class meats', whose family continue to operate the business from these premises today. A young lad with a large bucket and shovel can also be seen, no doubt collecting horse droppings for the garden!

Tooting police station shortly after it opened for business in June 1939. The five-storey building contained 1,130 rooms and was considered to be the most advanced of its type in the country. Plans for the station underwent extensive remodelling while the building was being erected to accommodate improved facilities for the air-raid precautions services as a result of the increasing threat of war.

THE ROYAL VISIT TO TOOTING

Amen Corner, 1923. Thousands of local residents throng the street to cheer King George V and Queen Mary on their drive through Tooting on Saturday 28 July after they had opened Southfields Park. Over 6,500 children from Balham, Tooting and Streatham were massed in Tooting Bec Road to welcome the royal visitors, spurred on by the Balham citadel band of the Salvation Army (see p. 79).

Amen Corner, c. 1912. The name probably derives from the ancient ceremony of 'beating' the parish bounds which used to end at this spot with the saying of a prayer to which the party would respond with a loud 'Amen!' The original Tooting police station is on the right; at present it serves as an office for the Wandsworth Council Interpreting Service.

Mitcham Road, *c.* 1930, looking towards Tooting from Amen Corner. St Boniface Church, built in 1907, had to wait until 1927 for the Byzantine frontage and bell tower to be added. The bell tower is now a prominent landmark. The only remaining house on the right is now used by the church.

St Nicholas Parish Church on its completion in 1833. In the following year the old Saxon church which possessed the last remaining round tower in Surrey was demolished. In this picture the old church is visible between the new church and the tree. In reality the old church stood much nearer Church Lane than depicted here. It was probably in existence in AD 675 when the first mention of Tooting is given in an old Saxon charter.

The Electric Pavilion cinema, 132 Mitcham Road, shortly before opening in 1914. Workmen are putting the final touches to this building which was built between Bickersteth Road and the Mitre public house. Today the Gateway supermarket occupies this site.

The Mitre public house, 16 August 1914. This old coaching inn, on the route into Surrey, was rebuilt in 1906. The pub was a popular starting point for charabanc outings. Here local children gather outside the Mitre, awaiting coaches to arrive for their day out. The old English word 'Ye' used in pub signs recalls the now defunct use of the letter Y which has now been replaced by our modern-day 'th'.

Mitcham Road, *c.* 1910. The Mitre public house is on the left, with the Congregational Church beyond. Note the cast-iron canopy entrance to the saloon bar, now sold off and used as a retail shop.

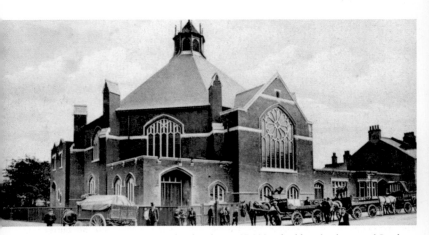

The Congregational Church, *c.* 1906. The church cost £7,000 to build to the designs of Gordon and Gunton. It was opened by Miss Miller who lived at Lynwood (a large house in Upper Tooting Road). The church roof, with six sides crowned by a lantern, was a distinctive feature in Mitcham Road. The building was demolished in 1988.

Mitcham Road, *c.* 1914, looking from the roof of The Foresters' Arms public house. The tower of St Nicholas Parish Church and the Surrey hills beyond Croydon are visible, as well as the Congregational Church.

Boys' Life Brigade, *c.* 1910. The Tooting company of the Boys' Life Brigade was founded by the Revd Bevill Allen, minister of the Congregational Church from 1893 until 1929. The company was one of the largest in the area and boasted a fine drum and bugle band, seen here. Note the 'Drum Majors' on either side of the group wearing their peaked hats and shining leather shoulder belts.

Mitcham Road, c. 1914. This is another view from the roof of The Foresters' Arms, this time looking down Mitcham Road towards the Broadway. The dome of the Methodist Central Hall tower can be seen above the skyline. In the background are the trees along Burntwood Lane and on the Springfield Estate. Shop blinds are out to protect goods on display from discoloration by the sunlight.

Mitcham Road, c. 1910. The pavements are crowded with shoppers and the wares of the local traders, such as rolls of linoleum and travelling cases. Note the tram stop on the lamp-post announcing that 'cars STOP here if required'. The poster above the Vant Road street sign advertises the train service from Paddington to Ireland via Fishguard operated by the GWR—The Great Western Railway, or as it was more popularly then known 'God's Wonderful Railway'.

Mitcham Road, 12 February 1926. The Library, which opened in November 1902, was presented to the people of Tooting by the mayor of Wandsworth, Sir William Lancaster. It originally comprised only one storey but was extended in 1908 when a second floor was built. The clock was added in 1906 to commemorate the work of the rector of Tooting and ex-mayor of Wandsworth, the Revd John Hendry Anderson. It cost £150 of which £100 was raised by public subscription.

The Granada, Mitcham Road, c. 1948. The Granada cinema, which opened on 7 September 1931, could accommodate up to 6,000 patrons and had seating for 4,000. Designed by M. Komisarjevski, it heralded in a new age in cinema architecture and was styled a 'Cathedral of the Talkies'. The first film screened was *Monte Carlo*, starring Jack Buchanan and Jeanette MacDonald. A seat in the stalls cost 6d before one o'clock, increasing to 8d and 1s 3d in the evenings. During the war a captured Heinkel bomber was displayed in the cinema's car park and an entrance fee of 6d adults and 3d children was charged to view it. The proceeds went towards the local Spitfire fund which was launched by Sir Alfred Butt, the local MP, with a donation of 100 guineas. Note the trolley bus in the centre of the picture. These were introduced locally in 1937 and were not withdrawn from service until 1962.

Harold Ramsay at the console of the 'Mighty Wurlitzer' at the Granada cinema in Tooting, c. 1935. He was one of the more famous of the cinema organists and was musical director for Union Cinemas, which operated the Ritz and Regal theatre chain. Harold was a Canadian by birth and returned to Canada at the beginning of the Second World War. The cinema is now a listed building and was converted into a bingo hall in 1976.

The Broadway Cinematograph Palace, 1912. The Broadway Palace was Tooting's first 'super' cinema when it opened in 1912. It was built by three partners, Browning, Hellier and Batley, and had 800 armchair tip-up seats to accommodate patrons. A pipe organ provided music to accompany the silent films and customers were served with a free cup of tea during the matinée programme. The 7 ft statue of Britannia that crowned the building was deemed to be unsafe in April 1949 and was removed. The cinema occupied the site formerly used by the Blunt family to market their flowers, plants and vegetables.

Laying the tram lines in Mitcham Road, 1907. Tooting had to endure extensive roadworks necessitated by the laying of the LCC tram tracks from Garratt Lane to Tooting Junction in 1907. The occasion was used to demolish several buildings in order to widen the road. Note the large number of cobbled stones piled up next to the wagon on the left of the picture.

Mitcham Road, c. 1910. A small group awaiting the tram to Mitcham or Streatham crowd the pavement corner at the junction of Mitcham Road and Tooting High Street. The enamel sign above the shop on the left points the way to Mitcham and identifies the area as 'Tooting Broadway SW'. In the distance the roof of the Congregational Church dominates the skyline.

Methodist Central Hall, *c.* 1911. Joseph Rank, the millionaire miller who lived in Bushey Down at the top of Church Lane, Tooting, donated £14,000 towards the £20,000 cost of the hall which was built on the site of Fairfield House. It was opened by Lady Brooks Marshall on 10 November 1910. The main hall could accommodate 1,800 people, with seating for an additional 800 persons being available in the lower hall. After the First World War a memorial tablet was set up in the entrance of the hall to commemorate sixty-eight young Tooting men who gave their lives in the conflict. The building was a popular venue for local concerts and talks. The hall was badly damaged by bombing in 1940 and was eventually demolished in 1967 to make way for a Marks and Spencer store.

Tooting Broadway, 1906. Before the statue of King Edward VII was erected a smaller statue of a child and a guardian angel surmounting a drinking fountain occupied the site next to the magnificent gas lamps on the central island. Most of the eighteenth-century buildings on the right of the photograph above were eventually demolished to make way for commercial development of the area. The photograph below shows the Broadway in about 1960, complete with the large Guinness clock above Barrington's the jewellers, which was a local landmark for many years. By this time the gas lamps had lost their globes, although these have recently been restored.

Statue of King Edward VII, *c.* 1920. The public contributed £715 *6s 9d* for the statue by L.F. Roselieb of Park Hill, Clapham Park. The statue shows the king dressed as Commander-in-Chief, one hand holding a Field Marshal's baton, the other resting on his sword. In 1994 the statue was moved nearer the entrance to Tooting Broadway station and positioned so as to face London as part of the renovation of Tooting Broadway by Wandsworth Council.

The unveiling of the statue of King Edward VII by Councillor Archibald Dawney, mayor of Wandsworth, on 4 November 1911. The occasion was one of great celebration and the Broadway was packed to capacity with Tooting residents. The large-brimmed hats of the local Boy Scouts can be seen at the front of the crowd, and the mayor's attendants, resplendent in their livery, are to the left of the statue.

Tooting Broadway flooded after the heavy fall of rain that occurred on 14 June 1914. On the left people can be seen perched under the awning of the Central Hall, while in the distance storm debris floats on the large sheet of water that surrounds the king's statue. The storm was the worst to hit Tooting in living memory and seven people were killed during the four-hour downpour when they were struck by lightning on Wandsworth Common.

The great storm, June 1914. The photograph above shows a large crowd gathered outside the dental surgery of Stewart and Douglas in Tooting High Street after the storm. Rain is still falling as a number of 'brollies are up, and the policeman is wearing his waterproof cape. On the left is a pile of debris which has been swept into the gutter in an effort to clear the road. The surrounding streets also experienced serious flooding during the storm. In Seely Road, below, three boys take the opportunity to paddle in the centre of the road.

Two

Tooting High Street and Upper Tooting Road

Tooting High Street, *c.* 1910. A London United tramways car No. 239, en route to Hampton Court, stands at the terminus. On the left, at the junction of the High Street and Blackshaw Road, a large board advertises J. Hyde's furniture shop. Above this building can be seen three large brass balls, signifying the location of the pawnbroker's shop. A notice in the windows below advises 'Money lent on Pianos'.

The Black Spot cinema, 181 Tooting High Street, c. 1914. The break in the row of tall terraced buildings on the right is occupied by the single-storeyed entrance lobby of the cinema. Known as the Gaiety cinema in 1922–3, it also traded as a confectioners. Palmer's Motor Engineering works is next door, closest to the camera.

No. 118 Tooting High Street, c. 1912. Two large dustbins rest on top of the awning cover of Spice's Household Domestic Stores. Outside the store William Spice has laid out his wares on the pavement to entice customers. On the corner of Hoyle Road an old hobby-horse 'bone-shaker' bicycle has been fixed above the door by Richard Jewell, the cycle dealer.

Convent of the Holy Family School at 85-99 Tooting High Street, *c.* 1906. The convent provided a boarding and day school for young girls. Although the school predominantly catered for girls (as the photograph below illustrates), it also taught young boys up to the age of ten years. The building used to be known as Merton House and is a fine example of Georgian architecture. For many years it was the home of Dr Samuel Bligh (1842–1925) and his son-in-law and successor, Dr Daniel Powell (1870–1938). Dr Bligh's wife, Eliza, who died in 1931 aged eighty-five, proudly boasted that she knew friends who had seen Lord Nelson and Lady Hamilton driving down Tooting High Street on their way to Merton.

Tooting Broadway tube station, *c.* 1928. The station was opened on 13 September 1926 and was built to the designs of S.A. Heaps, who was probably responsible for much of the interior detail, and Charles Holden, who designed the exterior, including the London Transport symbols which adorn the top of the columns over the entrance. The station is a listed building and was built on the site of a large house that used to be the residence of Mr James Fisher, auctioneer and property dealer (see p. 25).

Tooting High Street, *c.* 1910. Garratt Lane (formerly Defoe Road) is on the left, and the gentleman standing on the corner in a straw boater is outside Jung's bakery. Peter Jung operated his baker's shop in Tooting from 1890 to 1933, despite having his windows smashed several times during the First World War by angry crowds of anti-German protesters. His son, Peter junior, was awarded the British Empire Medal for his work with the National Savings movement.

The Defoe Primitive Methodist Chapel, 19 Tooting High Street, *c.* 1906. The chapel is said to date back to 1766, when it was built by Mrs Miles, the widow of a previous minister, to replace a wooden chapel erected on this site in 1688. This was founded as a Presbyterian meeting house supposedly by Daniel Defoe, the famous author of *Robinson Crusoe*. Despite a marked lack of documentary evidence to support this claim, the story has passed into local legend and is perpetuated in local street names such as Defoe Road (now Garratt Lane), Robinson and Selkirk Roads. The Methodists took the chapel over in 1904. Today the building has been converted into shops.

Upper Tooting Road, *c.* 1912. The dining rooms of Edward Tress stand proudly at the junction of Kellino Street and Upper Tooting Road; its smart blinds are partly drawn to protect its patrons from the bright sunshine. Next door, at William Spice's stores, a wide array of hardware and household goods adorn the shop, devoid of protection from the sun's rays.

Upper Tooting Road, c. 1910. The parade of shops between Broadwater Road and Moffat Road is dominated by the large clock which marks the location of Hasting's Furnishers at 234–40 Upper Tooting Road. Meanwhile, above Frederick Ogburn's baker's shop, a sign urges the residents of Tooting to 'Eat Ogburn's Bread'.

Upper Tooting Road, c. 1905. The first building on the left is The Bell Coffee Palace, which was built in 1888. It stands on the site of the former Bell public house, which was owned by St Leonard's Church, Streatham, as part of a charitable bequest made to the parish by Gabriel Livesay in 1628. Although the Bell has subsequently been demolished, the small terraced building next door survives today. A small square tablet set between the pair of windows on the first floor is still visible; it bears the initials HSE and the date 1822.

The King's Head, 84 Upper Tooting Road, *c.* 1909. The present building of 1896 replaces an earlier inn. This may be the one referred to as 'newly built' in 1620, where Mary Smith, 'a stranger', was born and whose baptism is recorded in the Streatham parish registers on 11 November 1635. In 1798 the tavern was described as 'a good accustomed house, with genteel accommodation and reasonable charges', and was the starting point for George Holden's stage-coach, which left there each morning at 8 a.m. bound for the Spread Eagle in Gracechurch Street.

Prince & Co., 9 Upper Tooting Road, *c.* 1908. Members of the Balham and Tooting Traders Association parade outside Prince's boot and shoe shop, at the corner of Dafforne Road and Upper Tooting Road, in an effort to encourage local residents to shop locally. Prince's was one of the largest shoe-shops in the area. Ladies could get their boots soled and heeled there for 1s 6d.

Upper Tooting Road, c. 1930. This view is graced by the impressive cupola which adorned the Central Hall Picture Palace, on the corner of Fircroft Road, and the building at the junction of Topsham Road. A member of staff from Cresswell and Matcham, piano manufacturers, is cleaning the windows of the works at the junction of Beechcroft Road. The block of shops between Fircroft and Mandrake Roads was erected between 1929 and 1930.

Central Hall cinema, c. 1930. This cinema was one of the earliest to be built in Tooting and dates from 1911. It later became the Classic cinema. Its fortunes, however, steadily declined until it was closed in 1986. Part of the building was subsequently converted into retail shopping units.

The first tram in Upper Tooting Road, 1903. The Prince of Wales (later to become King George V) rides atop the first LCC tram to run on the electrified line along Upper Tooting Road amid the cheers of thousands of local residents who thronged the route. The prince's journey marked the opening of the route between Westminster and Tooting on 15 May 1903. The prince's tramcar was painted white and elaborately decorated with garlands and palm leaves. The view below shows the interior of the car when it was taken to the Marius Road tram depot at Balham after its official run (see also p. 82).

Upper Tooting Road, 12 February 1926. Brudenell Road is the turning on the left. The sign for the King's Head public house can be seen in the middle of the picture, although the pub itself is not visible, being set back slightly from the right-hand side of the road. Note the large gaslight over the shop window on the right, the size of which was necessary in order to illuminate the window at night.

Trinity Road station, c. 1930. The underground railway was extended from Clapham to Morden in 1926 and this station was opened on 13 September of that year. Originally known as Trinity Road station, it was renamed Tooting Bec station in 1950. During 1994 it was completely refurbished, with new glass, signs and flagpoles. The Wheatsheaf public house, which was rebuilt in 1892, stands opposite. A building has stood on this spot since at least the seventeenth century, and an inn has refreshed local travellers here from the early 1700s. In 1822 a complaint was made against the then landlord, Michael Merrett, for allowing 'excessive tippling'.

Three

Tooting Streets

Beechcroft Road, *c.* 1919. This was part of the road between Upper Tooting Road and Glenburnie Road, formerly known as Obligation Row. In the 1890s eight terraces of houses were built there; these were called: Rusthall Villas, Cumberland Terrace, Cumberland Villas, Hampton Terrace, Spring Terrace, The View, Hyde Villas and Earl's Park Terrace. These names were abolished in July 1898 when the whole length of the street was renamed Beechcroft Road. St Peter's Presbyterian Church is on the left. Built in 1898, the church replaced a small iron chapel which had occupied the site since 1895. The iron building was used as a church hall until it was demolished in 1929 when the new hall was built.

Bickersteth Road, c. 1908. This old ivy-clad cottage used to stand at the junction of Bickersteth Road and Mitcham Road. A cow was kept in the back garden to provide the occupants with a regular supply of fresh milk, butter and cheese. Original houses in the road were given such rural names as Thanet Cottages, Florence Villas and Myrtle Villas, all of which were swept away at the turn of the century. By that time the road had lost most of its rural charm.

Brudenell Road, c. 1912. This was named in honour of Lord Charles William Brudenell-Bruce, whose widow financed the building of All Saints' Church which was consecrated in July 1906 (see p. 51). The church tower can be seen on the horizon. In front of the tower is a placard advertising for sale 'local villas from £250'. These were being erected on the Elmwood Estate by local builders Swain and Selly.

Grove Hospital, Blackshaw Road. The Grove Hospital for Infectious Diseases opened here on 17 August 1899. It was well established by the time the top photograph was taken of the Tooting Grove entrance in around 1912. During the First World War the building was used as an isolation hospital, and the photograph below shows soldiers in one of the wards in around 1915. The hospital was renamed St George's in 1954 and now forms part of the large complex which has been developed on the site following the transfer here of the major part of London's St George's Hospital and medical school in 1980.

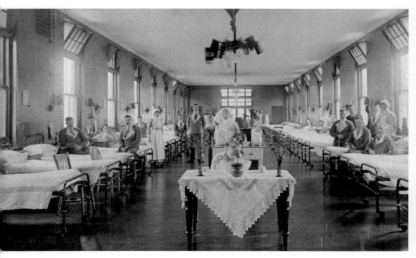

Church Lane, *c.* 1910. Lessingham Avenue is on the right, while the tower of St Nicholas' Church, after which the lane was named, can be seen at the bottom of the hill. When this photograph was taken the lane was still a dirt road, notoriously dusty in the hot summer months, and boggy and muddy in the winter. The rural aspect of the lane is evident from the stands of tall trees which line either side of the road.

Church Lane School, *c.* 1908. The Parochial School was erected in Church Lane in 1829. Repairs were needed in 1845 when it was discovered that the school had been built over a medieval moat, which had been poorly filled-in about twenty years earlier. The building eventually became the parish hall and is now used by the local Sikh community.

The Tooting Home, *c.* 1907. Originally built in 1888 as St Joseph's Catholic College, the building was purchased in 1895 by the Wandsworth Board of Guardians for use as a Home for the Aged Poor, called Tooting Home. During the First World War it became a military hospital which subsequently became St Benedict's Hospital (after it was purchased by the LCC in 1923 for use as a convalescent hospital). Tooting's first barrage balloon was sited here on 1 August 1939, but it had to be winched down as it interfered with the tower of the local parish church. Five wards at the hospital were badly damaged in 1944 by a V1 bomb that fell in nearby Freshwater Road. The building was demolished in 1985, but the clocktower survives today in Limetree Walk, where it was erected in the middle of the housing estate built on the site of the hospital.

Church Lane military hospital, *c.* 1916. Soldiers are warming themselves by the stove in the YMCA military hospital hut. This was erected in the grounds of the Tooting Home to accommodate wounded men during the First World War.

Clairview Road, *c.* 1908. Six large houses facing Tooting Graveney Common used to stand on this site. In one of these mansions, called Woodlands, lived Henry Doulton, the famous potter. He played an important role in preventing the enclosure of the Common in the 1860s. Doulton sold his house to Charles Derry, of Derry and Toms department store fame, who lived there until the house was demolished, along with its neighbours. Clairview Road was laid out on the site between 1906 and 1909.

Crowborough Road, *c.* 1926. This road was built on the grounds of Furzedown House. The first house was erected in 1905 and the last was finished in 1925. The last flying bomb to fall in Streatham exploded at the junction of Crowborough Road and Ramsdale Road on 13 August 1944.

Cromer Road on the Links Estate, c. 1912. All the roads off Links Road run in alphabetical order. Most were named after popular Edwardian holiday destinations, hence the third road starting with the letter C and christened Cromer after the Norfolk holiday town.

Eswyn Road, c. 1912. Developed from 1904 onwards, mainly by George Palmer and P.E. Miller, the road was named after the daughter of one of the developers. A former resident of the road was the Right Revd John Healy, who became the Roman Catholic Bishop of Gibraltar. He lived here as a young boy and attended Undine Street School. In 1944 houses in the road were damaged when a V1 bomb fell here.

Fircroft Road, *c.* 1925. Peter Dunican CBE is probably the road's most famous resident. He was a partner in Ove Arup, consulting engineers, and worked on the Sydney Opera House, the Crystal Palace sports centre, the Queen Elizabeth Hall and the Hayward Gallery. In 1896 Fircroft Road School was built, with accommodation for 884 pupils. The cupola of the Central Hall Picture Palace, at the junction of Upper Tooting Road, can be seen on the left at the bottom of the hill.

Foulser Road, *c.* 1912, laid out on the former estate of Sir William Rose, Lord Mayor of London in 1862–3. As Lord Mayor it fell on him to host a special Guildhall banquet in honour of the Prince and Princess of Wales on the occasion of their marriage. Sir William was an oil refiner based in the City and Conservative MP for Southampton from 1862 to 1868. His estate was developed from 1883 onwards. Today the gate lodge in Tooting Bec Road is all that remains of his estate; it is used as a garden centre.

Antcliffe's grocery shop, 844–6 Garratt Lane, c. 1914. Mr F.G. Antcliffe and his young assistant are standing in the doorway of his shop. On display in his neat but crowded windows are Hudson's soap, Limelight wax candles, Rova cocoa, Bivox beef tea, buttermilk soap and Juvis beef tea.

Gassiott Road, c. 1912. The road was named after Charles Gassiott, a successful London wine merchant, who lived at Elmwood House in Tooting. He was a generous local benefactor and gave the land on which All Saints' Church was built. He was also a keen art collector and left his paintings to the National Gallery and the Guildhall Art Gallery. He died a wealthy man, leaving almost £750,000, £250,000 of which he bequeathed to St Thomas's Hospital. His widow established a Tooting charity for the poor, which she endowed with £5,000 in her will.

Glasford Street, *c.* 1914. Two small hand-pulled baker's vans and a dairy cart, complete with a large metal milk churn, deliver fresh milk and bread to the residents. Delivering fresh food to the door was a common practice by local traders, even as late as the 1950s. Today the local milkman is the last vestige of this service.

Springfield Hospital, *c.* 1915. Built at a cost of £63,000 on grounds which once formed part of Springfield Farm, the hospital was originally known as the Surrey County Lunatic Asylum. The hospital was opened on 14 June 1841 with 299 patients, all of whom had been transferred from other institutions. The site has been significantly extended over the years. The original hospital is a listed building, as is the eighteenth-century ice-house which stands in the hospital grounds and once formed part of Springfield Farm.

No. 88 Himley Road, c. 1920. Mr Clark and his assistant stand outside his small grocery shop, which was located on the corner of Charlmont Road. The road was originally laid out in 1869 and formerly comprised some ten separate groups of villas and terraces, all of which were combined in July 1900 to form Himley Road.

Longley Road, *c.* 1910. Two of the road's most famous residents are commemorated by blue plaques. At No. 46 Sir Harry Lauder (1870–1950) resided from 1903 to 1911. He was a famous Scottish music-hall performer, well-known today for his renditions of 'Keep Right on to the End of the Road' and 'Roaming in the Gloaming'. The modern building erected on the site of No. 72 bears the plaque to mark the former residence there of Harry Tate (Richard Macdonald Hutchinson). He was a popular music-hall comedian who made famous the song 'Good-bye-ee'. His catch-phrase of 'How's Your Father?' has long passed into the popular vocabulary. He was born in Scotland in 1872 and died in 1940 from injuries he received in an air raid.

Harry Cusden's store at 183–9 Longley Road in about 1912, when a dozen bottles of whiskey cost 40s, and six bottles of Gilbey's gin would set you back 10s 6d.

Staff outings from Harry Cusden's stores in 1925 (top) and 1914 (bottom). Harry Cusden was a well-known local shopkeeper who started in business in 1893. By the mid-1920s he owned almost forty outlets across South London. His brother Jonathan started a chain of ironmonger's shops, eventually owning around seven shops in Wandsworth, Tooting and Norwood. None of the shops survives today.

Mantilla Road, c. 1910. This road was laid out on the Birbeck Estate in 1880, although most of the houses were not built until much later. An old LCC boundary post, marking the edge of Tooting Graveney Common, still stands on the left-hand side of the road at the junction with Church Lane. The houses at the south-eastern end of the road mark the garden boundary of Bushey Down, the former residence of Joseph Rank, the wealthy miller and keen supporter of Methodism in Tooting.

Moring Road, Birbeck Estate, c. 1910. The different styles of building in this road reveal the various phases of development. This originally comprised Cavendish Villas, Priory Gardens, The Gables and Abbey Gardens. Although children playing in Moring Road at this time did not have to fear the motor car, they did have to take care to avoid what horse-drawn traffic often left in the roadway!

Nimrod Road, *c.* 1914. This view shows the steepness of the hill leading down to the Wandle Valley. Nimrod Road was laid out in 1901, with the houses there built between 1902 and 1927. Jean Jacques Haakman, a famous Dutch maestro who had met Brahms, Lizst, Massenet, and other famous composers of the age, died here in February 1931. Another resident was Flying Officer Kenneth Ames, who was awarded the DFC in 1943 for successfully piloting his seriously damaged bomber back to the UK after a daring bombing raid on Kassell. In 1944 he received a bar to his DFC for his outstanding performance in bombing raids over Berlin.

All Saints' Church, *c.* 1912. This view shows the church surrounded by open fields before the developers had erected the adjacent roads of houses. Building work began on the church in 1904, and it was consecrated on 7 July 1906. Lady Brudenell-Bruce paid for the church to be built in memory of her husband (see p. 38). The magnificent-looking building to the left of the church is the vicarage, which was demolished in 1960.

Rectory Lane, c. 1906. Formerly known as Back Lane, this was one of the old trackways of Tooting village. The trees and shrubs on the Furzedown Estate line the right-hand side of the lane, while the old Tooting Home, later to become St Benedict's Hospital, can be seen through the trees on the left (see p. 41). This rural scene can easily be compared with the view below taken some fourteen years later. By this time Back Lane has become Rectory Lane, and the centuries-old dirt track has become a tarred road lined with smart new houses for the aspiring middle classes.

Seely Road, c. 1912. Young children gather outside the baker's shop of Holgate and Co., which can be seen in the foreground. At this time the road was still only partly built and construction work was continuing in the open fields stretching out towards Mitcham. The road was named after Sir Charles Seely (1833–1915), Member of Parliament for Nottingham, who used to reside at Furzedown.

Smallwood Road School, c. 1909. Young pupils at Smallwood Road School are suitably dressed to celebrate the May Festival, at which the May Queen is crowned and enthroned and sits in regal splendour in the centre of the back row. Smallwood Road School was built in 1898 to the designs of T.J. Bailey. The school buildings were extended in 1908 to accommodate the increasing number of young children in the neighbourhood.

Southcroft Road, *c.* 1912. For many years the absence of housing along Southcroft Road, which had panoramic views across the River Graveney to Figgs Marsh in Mitcham, led tram drivers to call this area 'The Prairie'. The junction with Mitcham Lane was a dangerous corner, and numerous tram accidents occurred here as drivers negotiated the bend at too fast a speed. The road was originally laid out in 1904 although house building was not completed until 1936.

Totterdown Street, *c.* 1907. At one time an old pump and drinking fountain stood here to quench the thirst of local residents. Frank Staff, former mayor of Wandsworth, used to tell an amusing story of how this street got its name from olden times when inhabitants used to cross Totterdown fields here, and in so doing had to traverse the narrow strips of cultivated land and literally 'tottered down' to Tooting! However, the name probably derives from old English and is a composite of 'Tot', a look-out place; 'aern', a house; and 'dun', a hill. This suggests the location of a possible look-out post, and may even refer to the old Saxon tower of the original St Nicholas Church.

Trinity Road, c. 1910. A blue plaque on No. 172 commemorates the former residence of the famous author Thomas Hardy (1840–1928). He lived here between 1878 and 1881, at which time the house was known as The Larches, No. 1 Arundel Terrace. While living here Hardy wrote *The Trumpet Major*, published in 1880, and *A Laodicean*, published in 1881. Another famous resident commemorated by a plaque is the former prime minister, David Lloyd George, who resided at No. 193 between 1900 and 1904. In the centre of the bottom picture is an old fire-alarm post, standing next to the telegraph post at the junction with St James Drive.

Trinity Road police station, *c.* 1910. The plot of ground on which the station stands was purchased in 1883, although the building was not completed until 1886. The station closed in 1972, but increased crime in the Balham area forced it to reopen in December 1985 and ensured that it celebrated its centenary the following year. Fred Cherrill started his career at this station as a young PC pounding the Balham beat, rising through the ranks to become a Chief Superintendent and head of Scotland Yard's fingerprint section, and one of Britain's leading criminologists. He retired from the force in 1953.

Holy Trinity Church and Trinity Road fire station, *c.* 1910. Holy Trinity Church was opened on 26 June 1855 by Bishop Charles Sumner. It cost £6,000 and originally provided accommodation for 722 worshippers. The building was enlarged and the tower added in 1860. Trinity Road was known as Wandsworth Lane up until 1879, when the name was changed as more people travelled the route to the church than to Wandsworth, particularly on a Sunday! The LCC fire station moved here from Balham High Road in 1907; the station was officially opened on 27 February 1908. It was kitted out with the most modern appliances of the day, including a new 'motor steamer', and boasted of being able to turn out for a fire within 30 seconds!

Four

Tooting Bec Common

Tooting Bec Common, *c.* 1910. Young children join hands around a bush while a small girl in a white smock looks on. The common has always been a popular place to play and most photographs at this time feature young children. They can be seen accompanied by their parents on Sunday afternoon walks, or playing by themselves or with their friends. There was always plenty to do on the common, from making camps in the shrubs to climbing trees. Cricket, with a tree as a wicket, and football, with two coats marking the goal mouth, were favourite sports, and games of tag or hide and seek in the bushes were also popular. The autumn months always had the added advantage of offering a rich picking of blackberries for eager young fingers.

The lake, Tooting Bec Common. The photograph above shows a typical Sunday afternoon sight in 1908, when families would dress up in their Sunday best and promenade along the various walks that crisscross the common. The lake was a popular spot to rest, and often boys could be seen here floating boats on the open expanse of water. The many feet that strolled round the lake is indicated by the vast expanse of grass that has been eroded away around the edge of the lake. During the winter it was not unusual for the lake to freeze over, when the chance would be taken for skating, as shown in the picture below taken during the winter of 1911/12.

The fossilized tree, *c.* 1910. The trunk of a fossilized tree used to stand close to the lake. Protected behind iron railings, it was a popular curiosity. The notice reads 'Fossilized remains of a tree trunk from the lower Purbeck bed, Portland; moved from Bedford Hill Park by the Balham Antiquarian and Natural History Society and placed here by the permission of the London County Council'.

The boating lake, *c.* 1916. This was a popular attraction on the common. In the summer months, particularly at weekends, the boating lake was packed with small rowing boats and paddle craft, which could be hired from the boatman.

The horse ride, c. 1912. A horse ride existed on the common and was a popular pastime. In fact, the number of riders galloping all over the common in the 1880s caused concern and led to the Streatham Vestry presenting a request to the Metropolitan Board of Works to restrict horse riding to an area of about 15 acres on the right and left of Tooting Bec Road. The closure of many of the local riding stables over the past ten years has led to fewer riders using the common and they are now a rare sight, yet they were relatively commonplace as recently as the mid-1980s.

Sunday strollers, c. 1912. Dr Johnson Avenue is on the left and was a favourite parade ground on Sunday afternoons. Then, top hats and straw boaters were the order of the day for the men, and the ladies wore long flowing dresses and carried parasols. For children, it was the time for pretty dresses or navy suits. A young boy wearing the latter can be seen in the middle of this photograph.

Two boys quenching their thirst at the old drinking fountain on the common, c. 1907. In 1938 a new drinking fountain was erected near the junction of Dr Johnson Avenue and Tooting Bec Road in memory of Joseph James Jones. He lived in Streathbourne Road and died in September 1931, leaving £24,000 in his will to fund a trust to encourage the playing of organized games by boys of local schools.

Boy Scouts on the common, c. 1910. Members of the local youth groups often used to meet on the common for organized games and activities. They were taught woodcraft and studied natural history. Here the local Scout troop are parading complete with their drum and bugle band. The Wandsworth Battalion of the Boys' Brigade also used to regularly assemble on the common for their annual parade, when their column would march off to a local church headed by the massed band of the battalion.

Dr Johnson's Avenue, c. 1909. A horse-drawn milk cart makes its way through the snow along Dr Johnson Avenue. The rustic bridge over the small stream, which used to flow alongside the avenue, can be seen on the right. This stream, known locally as York Ditch, was part of the old Falcon Brook, one of the many tributaries of the River Thames, and marks the boundary between the parishes of Streatham and Tooting Graveney.

The kiosk, c. 1907. The tea kiosk has always been a popular spot for refreshment. It provided Sunday strollers with a focal point to aim for, where the cup that cheers could be enjoyed before setting off on the walk home.

Tooting Lido, *c*. 1912. Tooting Lido was built by the London County Council at a cost of £7,700 and was opened on 28 July 1906. At that time it was one of the largest outdoor swimming pools in the country. It quickly became the base for the South London Swimming Club, which is famous for holding its Christmas Day dips here, regardless of the weather! The pool was modernized in 1931 when dressing cubicles and a filtration house with fountain were added. Note the LCC rescue rowing boat tied up by the left-hand side of the diving board.

The railway cutting, *c*. 1904. Rastrick, a class B2 locomotive built in 1896 by the London, Brighton and South Coast Railway, pulls the Waterloo to South Coast train along the track crossing Tooting Bec Common. The loco was originally painted in the 'improved green' livery (actually an orange-yellow shade), and was repainted dark green in 1905. The engine was rebuilt in 1910 and was in use until 1930 when it was withdrawn from service.

Tooting Bec Road and the asylum. Built on the site of Tooting Lodge, the manor house for Tooting Graveney, the asylum was opened in 1903 by the Metropolitan Asylum Board to cater for 1,000 patients. In 1912 Bushey Down—the home of Joseph Rank, the millionaire miller – wa purchased for £10,000 for the extension of the hospital. However, the First World War delayed this work and it was not completed until 1925, when capacity was increased to accommodate 2,200 patients. The hospital is now facing closure and the future of the site is uncertain. Part of the television drama *Selling Hitler*, the story of the fake Hitler diaries, was filmed here. The photograph above shows the asylum in around 1909; below is the view along Tooting Bec Road towards the railway bridge in around 1919.

Five

Balham High Road

No. 215 Balham High Road, c. 1911. This impressive-looking house was for many years the Wandsworth Borough Engineer and Surveyor's office, seen here suitably decorated for the coronation of King George V and Queen Mary. Prior to its use by the Council, it was a private residence known as Broxash; in 1894 it was the home of a Mrs Wickens. It is typical of the many large houses that used to front Balham High Road before the area was developed with shops and other commercial buildings.

The old Tooting fire station, Balham High Road, *c.* 1905. The fire-escape ladder is parked on the pavement outside. In 1880 two horses were supplied to the station to pull the fire tender at a cost of £2 5*s* a week, and the Metropolitan Board of Works agreed to provide a coachman at a cost of £1 4*s* 6*d* a week (see p. 56). On the right is the old Methodist chapel on the site of which St Anselm's Church was built.

St Anselm's Church and convent, *c.* 1934. St Anselm's moved here in 1905, although the present building dates from 1933. In 1955 the abbot of the Abbey of Bec in Normandy visited St Anselm's as a guest of the then priest, Father LeWarne. The Abbey of Bec formerly owned the manors of Tooting and Streatham, and Tooting adopted the 'Bec' suffix to distinguish it from the neighbouring manor of Tooting Graveney.

French's Motor Engineering Works Ltd, 279–91 Balham High Road, *c.* 1926. Short Brothers of Northern Ireland started life as balloon manufacturers in 1906, with works in some railway arches at Battersea. In 1908 they began to build aeroplanes, and in 1909 French's transported a plane built by them from Olympia to the Isle of Sheppey. It measured 40 ft x 8 ft x 8 ft, and was believed to have been the largest item ever transported on British roads at that time. During the 1970s this building was the UK headquarters of Hertz Rent-A-Car – the largest car-hire company in the world.

No. 246 Balham High Road, *c.* 1912. The tall trees on the left shield the large houses that once stood on this stretch of the High Road from prying eyes. They were swept away, together with the houses, to make way for Du Cane Court which was built in the mid-1930s. It is the largest single block of flats under one roof in Europe. The estate comprises some 647 luxury apartments and was named after the Du Cane family, the owners of the land on which the development took place.

Troops parade past the post office at No. 256 Balham High Road, *c.* 1930. The unit was probably marching to or from the territorial headquarters located at 213 Balham High Road, which today is the base of C (City of London) Company of the 5th Battalion of the Royal Regiment of Fusiliers.

St Mary's Church, *c.* 1906. The nave of the present church dates from 1808, when it was opened as a proprietary chapel to St Leonard's Church, Streatham. Transepts were added in 1824; a chancel and apse followed between 1881 and 1882; with the addition of the domed baptistry, tower, belfry and new front in 1903 to 1904. The building was consecrated on Queen Victoria's birthday, 24 May 1855. Note the road-sweeper on the right, pushing his Wandsworth Borough Council dustcart No. 37.

Balham Conservatoire of Music, c. 1906. Located at Schiller House, 220 Balham High Road, this was established in 1900 under the proprietorship of Madame Kate Webb. Part of St Mary's Church can be seen to the right.

Balham High Road, c. 1906. Two LCC class A trams are collecting passengers just before Balham Railway bridge. The open-top trams were very popular in the hot summer months, but less so in the wet and windy winter ones. The authorities were soon persuaded to install an upper roof on these models to protect travellers from the elements.

Balham High Road, *c.* 1914. This row of shops, called Station Parade, was built in 1904. The London Joint City and Midland Bank occupied the corner site at the junction of Ravenstone Street. The Palladium cinema can be seen at the end of the block (see below).

The Palladium cinema, *c.* 1915. Built in 1914 between Balham station and Oakmead Road, this was a popular entertainment venue for local residents. The cinema would often change its programme three times a week so that patrons could attend regularly without seeing the same film twice. The cinema is screening *A Noble Sacrifice* and *At the Sign of the Lost Angel*. A forthcoming attraction is *The British Army Film*, recently shown by Royal Command. The Palladium was destroyed by bombing in the Second World War.

Balham station, c. 1906. Thomas Tilling's smart horse-drawn bus stands outside Balham station waiting passengers to ferry to Clapham Junction. A number of rival firms operated from this spot, and a horse-drawn vehicle of one operator or another seemed always to be waiting here for passengers. The station was originally built on the other side of the High Road and opened on 1 December 1856. It moved to its present position in 1863. Between 1927 and 1969 the station was known as Balham and Upper Tooting. The adjacent row of single-storey shops was demolished in the mid-1920s to make way for Balham underground station.

Balham underground station, c. 1935. This was opened on 6 December 1926 following the extension of the Northern Line to Morden. Unquestionably, one of the worst incidents of the Second World War to occur in Balham took place here. On the night of 14 October 1940 a bomb fell on the High Road above the station. It ruptured the water main and flooded the station, where a large number of people were sheltering from the raid. Sixty-eight people lost their lives in the incident.

Balham station. The photograph above shows the station in around 1922, by which time the old horse-drawn buses had been replaced by motorized taxi cabs. The photograph below shows some of the station staff standing on the Up platform in about 1900. Over the stationmaster's left shoulder can be seen the old signal-box, which was demolished in 1952. W.H. Smith's well-stocked kiosk can also be seen, crammed with papers, magazines and books. The station was largely rebuilt after the Second World War. The rebuilding began in 1949, but it was not in fact completed until around 1957.

The Balham engine, c. 1910. The driver and fireman peer from the footplate of this London, Brighton and South Coast Railway class D engine named in honour of Balham. It was used for the LBSCR's suburban services during the last quarter of the nineteenth century (see also p. 10).

Balham intermediate signal-box during the railway strike of 1911. A series of labour disputes in the docks and coalmines, which led to injuries and even deaths, convinced the government of the need to protect vital facilities. Troops and police were detailed to guard all signal-boxes for the safety of those continuing to work. The railway strike started on 13 August, with men returning to work on 21 August.

Balham High Road, c. 1928. This parade of shops was demolished and rebuilt following the disastrous bomb incident on 14 October 1940 (see p. 71). Note the fine gas lamp-posts on the corner of the High Road and Chestnut Grove on the left.

Balham High Road, c. 1913. The single-storey parade of shops on the right was built at the end of the nineteenth century on the front gardens of the houses originally erected here between 1840 and 1860. On the left-hand side of the road can be seen a brewer's horse-drawn cart laden with huge casks of beer, no doubt destined for a nearby pub. Note Pyke's cinema, which is visible beyond the cart.

Pyke's cinematograph, *c.* 1912. This was Balham's first purpose-built cinema and was opened in 1911. Seats were available for as little as 3*d.* It changed ownership on several occasions; subsequently it was known as the Rex, the Picture House and the Ritz. It ended its life as an Asian cinema before it was finally pulled down in 1985.

Balham High Road, *c.* 1912. The unusual clock and figures adorned the premises of J. W. Clark, pawnbroker. Either side of the bell stands old father time and an imperial-looking knight, resplendent in armour, ready to strike out the hours. Holdron's department store can be seen on the other side of the road.

Holdron's department store, *c.* 1912. This was one of Balham's premier stores and encompassed property either side of Balham Grove. Many of the staff who worked in the shop lived above the premises. This parade of shops was subsequently demolished and a Safeway supermarket now occupies the site. Bedford Hill is to the right.

Balham High Road, *c.* 1912. The London County Bank is on the left. Today this building is occupied by the National Westminster Bank. All the popular stores of the day occupied premises in this stretch of the High Road, including the Home and Colonial Stores, Liptons, and Freeman, Hardy and Willis. Near the tram was the De Luxe theatre, later used as the Empire cinema.

The old Balham post office, *c.* 1912. The building centre left was the old Balham post office, which was demolished in the early 1970s and rebuilt set back from the pavement. Chocolate is available from James, confectioners, on the left, at 8*d* per pound and the Ten Per Cent wine stores, next door, is offering Burgundy wine at 1*s* a bottle.

Balham High Road, *c.* 1906. Old Devonshire Road is to the right. All the shops fronting the left-hand side of the road were demolished following extensive bomb damage during the Second World War. The magnificent dome of the Duchess Palace theatre dominates the skyline at the far end of the road. Note the elaborate gas lamps on the right hanging in front of the Duke of Devonshire public house.

The Duke of Devonshire, 39 Balham High Road (on the corner of Balham New Road), *c.* 1906. This pub probably existed in the late eighteenth century. It was granted a lease in 1827, and was assigned to Young and Bainbridge in 1832, who have owned the pub ever since. In 1857 the brewers described it as a 'very valuable house' doing 'a large and increasing trade'. It was tenanted by George Lilly at £60 per annum, although the brewers thought it was worth twice this sum!

Walker and Sons dairy cart, *c.* 1907. Mr Walker and his sons operated their dairy business from 257 Balham High Road. Milk was delivered to the doorstep daily, and sometimes even twice daily to larger premises. Lack of refrigeration in private households meant frequent deliveries. Local authorities had to constantly check the quality as many small concerns would water the milk down to help boost profits. Young boys would frequently turn on the churn tap for devilment, when the milkman was not looking, and he would fly into a rage when he noticed the white gold wasting away along the gutter.

Balham Salvation Army band, c. 1908. The Balham corps was originally located on the corner of Balham High Road and Balham New Road before moving to the old Balham Assembly Rooms at 38 Balham High Road. This was reopened as the Congress Hall by Mrs Bramwell Booth. The Booths had a strong family connection with Balham as the first officer in charge at the Congress Hall was Colonel Bernard Booth, the grandson of the founder of the movement. The hall was badly damaged by a flying bomb in 1944. It was rebuilt in 1957 at a cost of £60,000.

Balham High Road and Balham Hill, c. 1910. The row of single-storeyed buildings marks the start of Balham High Road and for many years was occupied by John Newman, who ran a successful furniture and upholsterer's business from numbers 1 to 7. A wide range of furnishings was made on the premises, ranging from easy chairs and settees through to dining suites and bookcases. The first shop in Balham Hill, next to Newman's, belonged to Fred Barker who ran a hatter's, hosier's and shirtmaker's business here. The Duchess Palace theatre can be seen on the left.

W. Nottingham, ironmonger, 62 Balham High Road, *c.* 1908. Nottingham's sold a wide variety of household products, including china, glass, earthenware, brushes and brooms, buckets and pails, indeed everything the modern scullery or kitchen maid needed to do her chores. For a number of years the business was managed by William Duffield.

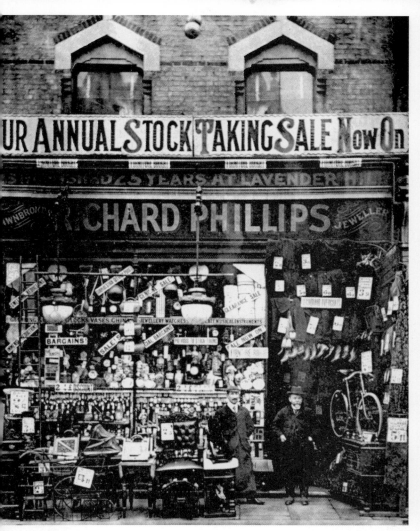

Richard Phillips, pawnbroker and jeweller, 21 Balham High Road, *c.* 1908. The business was still in operation in 1924, by which time it was owned by J.J. Barrett and Sons. The window is crowded with goods, no doubt including a large number of unclaimed pledged items. Many bargains were to be had: trousers at 3*s* 9*d* a pair, a velvet rug for 5*s*, an upholstered chair for 2*s* 3*d*, and an old pram for 4*s* 11*d*.

The opening of the LCC electric tramway, 1903. HRH The Prince of Wales passes along Balham High Road while inaugurating the electric tram service on 15 May 1903 (see also p. 35). The citizens of Balham have spared no expense to decorate their buildings with flags and bunting to welcome the prince, and the road is crammed with cheering crowds. The photograph below shows the prince's tram-car, complete with the Prince of Wales' feathers and decorative garlands. The car was probably at the Marius Road tram depot in Balham after its inaugural run.

Six

Balham Hill

The Duchess Palace, on the corner of Balham and Yukon Road, *c.* 1906. The Royal Duchess Theatre was opened on 18 September 1899 with a performance of *The Geisha*, starring Hayden Coffin. The building, which was constructed entirely of stone, was designed by William Sprague and cost £35,000 to build. It was crowned with a magnificent green copper dome, surmounted by a cupola on which was poised a classical winged figure. Attached to the colonnade, 110 ft above the pavement, was a powerful searchlight that sent out coloured beams. It was later known as the Balham Hippodrome and up to 2,500 patrons came here between the wars to see such stars of the day as Sophie Tucker and Billie Williams. The building was badly damaged by a bomb in the war and was subsequently demolished. Today a large block of flats occupies the site.

The Hippodrome and Balham Hill, *c.* 1912. The classical figures gracing the pediments of the Hippodrome peer down into the front gardens of the large houses which lined Balham Hill at the turn of the twentieth century. These were soon to be swept away in favour of commercial development. Note the two men in white coats cleaning the first-floor windows of one of the shops near the theatre.

Balham Hill, *c.* 1910. The winged effigy above the Hippodrome, welcoming visitors to Balham, quickly became a well-known local landmark. On the left are the gates to the yard of Young and Co., ironmongers and builders' merchants. A builders' merchant's business still operates from this site today. Next door, a hoarding advises that 'This Excellent Residence to be Let'.

The George Hotel, 16 Balham Hill, 1914 (above) and 1908 (below). Edwin Richard Coles, the proprietor, held the licence from 1905 to 1924. The George has occupied this site since the eighteenth century. It was originally established in 1715 on the other side of the road, but moved to its present location when it was first rebuilt in 1778 by a Mr Waring. It was briefly known as The George and Dragon in 1786. The George was a well-known coaching stop on the London Road, and as traffic grew so the business became more profitable. It was rebuilt for a second time in 1888 when the grand building seen here was erected, complete with a water trough so that horses could quench their thirst while their owners went inside to do the same.

Balham Hill, *c.* 1912. The Balham Hill Motor and Engineering Works at 117–23 Balham Hill can be seen on the right. Previously known as the Waldorf Motor Works (see p. 90), this was one of the earliest motor garages to be established on Balham Hill. It supplied early pioneering motorists with oil and petrol, and frequently, no doubt, helped them undertake emergency repairs to their newfangled machines.

Balham Hill, *c.* 1908. In the centre, next to the pillar-box, is an old fire alarm post. These posts were positioned at strategic locations so that, in the days before telephones were widely available, residents could quickly summon a fire engine in the event of an emergency. Although the windows of Freeman, Hardy and Willis at 63 Balham Hill, on the corner with Cathles Road, are crammed with shoes at discounted sale prices, the bargains don't seem to be drawing large crowds to the shop. Next door is W. J. Boyes (see opposite).

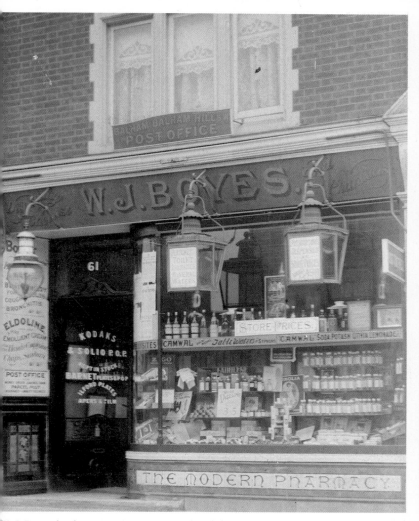

W. J. Boyes, the chemist, *c. 1908.* W.J. Boyes founded his business at 61 Balham Hill in 1895, and it still operates today from the same premises, although the Boyes family sold out over twenty years ago. In 1908 Mr Boyes also ran the Balham Hill post office from these premises. The ceramic tiles beneath the windows declare the shop to be 'The Modern Pharmacy', and all manner of pills and potions are displayed in the window, including 'Eldoline—a pure emollient cream ideal for hands and complexion, chaps and sunburn'.

Balham Hill, *c.* 1910. The parade of shops between Gaskarth and Hazelbourne Roads is on the right, the first four of which were called Grand Parade. There is a hairdresser's shop beyond the ladders, where a shave could be had for 2*d* and a haircut was a snip at 4*d*. Westbury Parade and Clapham South underground station was built on the site of the houses on the left-hand side of the road (see below).

Westbury Parade and Clapham South underground station, *c.* 1948. The station was opened on 13 September 1926. It was designed by Charles Holden and is similar in style to others built on the Morden line, such as Tooting Bec and Tooting Broadway. Westbury Parade, a large block of luxury flats, was built over the station in 1937. Nightingale Lane is to the right.

The South London Hospital for Women. Queen Mary opened the hospital on 4 July 1916 using a steel key—a sign of the wartime economy drive! The hospital was intended for women and children only. It was staffed and administered entirely by women, and was financed by voluntary donations. The photograph above shows the building in about 1916, prior to its enlargement in the 1930s. The view below shows the eighteen beds in the hospital's surgical ward in the early 1930s. The hospital was closed in 1984 and still stands empty ten years later, its future uncertain.

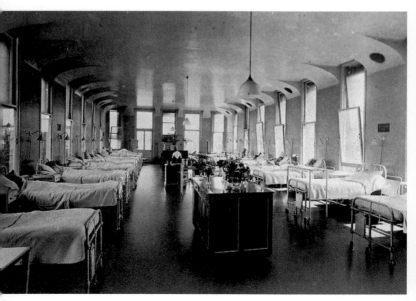

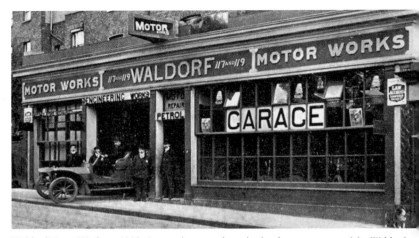

Waldorf Motor Works, c. 1908. A recently repaired car slowly edges its way out of the Waldorf Motor Works at 117–19 Balham Hill, while a number of local bystanders look on. Even the dog on the right considers the event worthy of attention (see also p. 86).

Charabanc outing to Brighton, c. 1920. Members of a pub, club, or company outing sit aboard an AEC charabanc parked in Cavendish Road, near the corner of South Side Clapham Common, before setting off for a day out to Brighton. It would have been a shaky ride down the A23 with only the vehicle's solid rubber tyres to absorb the bumps in the road. Such outings were commonplace between the wars and the old-fashioned charabancs remained popular until they were superseded by more substantial coaches. The later coaches also had the advantage of a roof to protect travellers in wet weather, rather than the folded hood seen at the rear of this vehicle!

Seven

Bedford Hill

The Priory, 225 Bedford Hill, c. 1906. The Priory gained notoriety in 1876 when it was the scene of the death of Charles Bravo by antimony poisoning. Suspicion fell on his wife, Florence, who had been carrying on an affair with the family physician, Dr Gully. The first inquest was inconclusive, but the second inquest, held at the Bedford Hill Hotel, returned a verdict of murder. However, no charges were ever laid and mystery still surrounds the incident today. As with the Jack the Ripper case, many theories as to the murderer have been proffered over the years, and numerous books have been written on the subject. The Priory was built in 1811, when it was known as Bedford Grove. The first inhabitant was a Mr Parkinson, followed by Henry Rucker who lived there between 1814 and 1830. The Bravos took up residence in 1874, but following Charles's death the house remained empty until 1890. Between 1892 and 1905 it was used as Harlington School, and in the 1930s it was converted into flats. By the early 1980s the by then dilapidated building was completely renovated and converted into luxury flats and survives today as a listed building.

Bedford Hill, *c*. 1911. The photograph above shows the Bedford Hill junction with Balham High Road. Rival milk carts can be seen either side of the road, with the milkman and milkboy eyeing each other suspiciously. On the left, carcases of meat can be seen hanging above the butcher's shop which was owned by Augustus C. Gifford. The view below shows Harberson Road, on the left, with Bedford Corn Stores occupying the corner premises. Here birdseed was going 'cheap' at just 1½*d* a pint! At the junction with Shipka Road is the recently converted corner shop which was turned into the Bedford Hill cinema in 1911. The cinema accommodated 100 patrons with seats available at 1*d* and 2*d*. The venture was short-lived, however, and by 1920 the building was being used as St Philip's Church Mission.

Balham market. The photograph above shows the area surrounding Balham market in around 1929. This has always been a busy and bustling centre for local traders. On the left, stall-holders have their wares laid out for public view along Hildreth Street, while on the right, an indoor market, called the Balham Covered Retail Market, was opened in 1925. The photograph below, taken in 1950, shows two of the traders, resplendent in white aprons, standing in front of their impressive display of canned produce. The distinctive striped livery of the market building, at the junction of Shipka Road, is clearly visible.

The Bedford public house, c. 1913. The photograph above shows Rossiter Terrace, a row of shops running between Rossiter Road and Fernlea Road. The corner premises is occupied by The Rossiter Laundry Company. In the distance, and below, is the Bedford public house, where the inquest on Charles Bravo was held in 1876 (see p. 91). The pre-First World War overhead electrification of the suburban train service can be seen running over the railway bridge. This was ultimately removed when the line was electrified using a third rail which was laid alongside the original track.

edford Hill, at the Larch Road junction, *c.* 1912. In February 1914 a strange discovery was made
one of the houses just past Elmfield Road. Workmen unearthed the skull and bones of a baby
nder the floorboards of the house. The remains had lain there for around twenty years and the
rcumstances of the burial remain as much a mystery today as they did then.

John's Church, *c.* 1920. The land for this church was donated by Mr James Brand, a director
the first telegraph company, who lived at Bedford Hill House. A temporary iron chapel stood
re for a couple of years before building work began on the church in 1883. The church was
signed in thirteenth-century Gothic style and was built of red and yellow bricks with stone
essings. By the late 1980s the building had become derelict and refurbishing was started on the
e in the autumn of 1994.

Bedford Hill, c. 1912. Veronica and Ritherdon Roads are on the left with St John's Church in the distance. No. 168, on the corner of Ritherdon Road, was for some years used as Bedford Hill College, and at No. 141, on the opposite side of the road, lived Dr Gully (see p. 91).

Bedford Hill, Balham.

Bedford Hill, c. 1908. This view shows Bedford Hill as it crosses Tooting Bec Common. The last house on the left (with the tower) was known as Culverdon. It was built in the late 1880s and provided a familiar landmark for those traversing the common.

Eight

Balham Streets

Cavendish Road, *c.* 1910. Formerly known as Dragmire Lane, part of the road marks the old parish boundary between Clapham and Streatham and therefore suggests that this may be a trackway of some antiquity. Cavendish House stood facing Clapham Common at the end of the road. Here lived the wealthy, eccentric, eighteenth-century scientist Henry Cavendish (1731–1810), in honour of whom the road was named in 1892. He was an eminent physicist, chemist and philosopher, and is widely recognized as the first man to convert oxygen and hydrogen into water, the discoverer of nitric acid, and the man 'who weighed the world'. He left his vast fortune, totalling £1,175,000, to his cousin, Lord George Cavendish.

Alderbrook Road, *c.* 1912. The road was laid out in 1878 and was named after a nearby stream which had alder trees growing alongside it. William A. De Jong, Deputy Superintendent Registrar of births, deaths and marriages for Wandsworth lived at No. 44, and Walter Hann, a famous scene painter, who did the scenery for the first stage production of J.M. Barrie's *Peter Pan* died at No. 2 on 16 July 1922 aged eighty-four.

Badminton Road, *c.* 1912. The large Edwardian houses in this road were only about five years old when this photograph was taken. At this time members of the Jekyll family were living at Nos 3, 17 and 23, although there is no trace of a Mr Hyde!

Balham Park Road, c. 1911. The photograph above shows a road-sweeper hard at work, but at least he has no parked cars in his way to impede his progress! Note also the ornate cast-iron railings surmounting the garden walls. A small acting school was set up here in 1978, run by Peter Bridgmont, who played in the opening production of *The Mousetrap*, as well as appearing in *Mrs Dale's Diary* and *Z Cars*. Mr C.J. Knight, Beadle of the City of London for thirty-four years, died at his son's house in Balham Park Road in 1935.

Blandfields Street, c. 1914. This street dates from 1897. Blandfields Stores was located at No. 42, which for a number of years at the turn of the century was owned by Joseph Down. At about the time this photograph was taken Mr T.F. Spencer was operating a laundry at Nos 14–16 and Miss M. Anderson was running the confectioner's and tobacconist's shop.

Brodrick Road, c. 1912. This road originally comprised some four groups of houses called Leicester, Hilperton, Norfolk and South Villas. These subsidiary names were abolished in 1890 when the road was renumbered. Brodrick Road is named after William Brodrick (c. 1558–1620), embroiderer to King James I, who lived in Wandsworth Town and owned a considerable amount of land in the area. St Mary Magdalene Parish Room and Library were located here.

Boundaries Road, c. 1908. This was named after the boundary between the parishes of Streatham and Battersea which ran along part of this road. This view, looking from the railway bridge towards Balham Park Road, shows the Trinity Baptist Chapel next to George Godfrey's builders' yard, in which a number of large pipes have been stacked. Further down the road, at No. 20, can be seen the works of the South Western Sanitary Laundry, which survives today as the Smart's Laundry Group. Soap and suds, together with a good deal of elbow grease, have been getting washing clean on this site for over a hundred years.

Bracken Avenue, c. 1914. Building work on the houses at the far end of this road was still under way when this photograph was taken shortly before the First World War. The road is named after a large Victorian house called The Brackens, which stood near this site on Nightingale Lane.

Cambray Road, c. 1910. The LCC named this road in 1898 and most of the houses had been completed so their occupants could celebrate the start of the twentieth century. The road was laid out on part of the Hyde Farm athletic ground, formerly one of Balham's oldest farms which was known to have existed in 1594, when it was leased by Robert Forth, and recorded in 1629 when some 61 acres were under cultivation.

Childebert Road, c. 1913. Clara Lowe, daughter of Lieut. General Sir Hudson Lowe, governor of Saint Helena during the time of Napoleon's imprisonment there, lived at No. 8 Childebert Road, where she died in May 1904 aged eighty-five. No. 74 was the residence of Henry Thomas Armfield, an eminent clergyman and scholar and former vice-principal of Sarum Theological College.

Chestnut Grove, 1912. The photograph above shows the Balham Hotel, on the corner of Boundaries Road. The first licence for this pub was granted to George Lilley in 1865 and he remained the proprietor until 1892 when George Huntley took over. The row of shops leading up to the pub includes L.A. Alfred's confectioners at No. 5; Charles Spiers' oil and colour (paint) and hardware stores; Henry Allanson, stationer; Mrs E. Connelly, draper; L.B. Whiles, fruiterer; C.C. Pinchard, watch-maker; Walter Smith's dining rooms; and Charles J. Smith, butcher at No. 9. The view below shows Gosberton Road, on the left, and Nightingale Square in the distance. It was photographed on Thursday 4 April 1912, as the notice to the right advises that 'this evening' Nos 60 and 62 Chestnut Grove were to be auctioned for sale by Mr Charles Hall.

Cornford Grove, c. 1912. George William Philips lived at No. 31. He was one of the founder members of the Balham Constitutional Club, and was the first chairman, holding the post for fifteen years. He also founded the Wandsworth Ratepayers Association in 1895, and was a member of Wandsworth Vestry where he served on the Building Committee. As a young man he joined the Special Constabulary in 1887 and received a commendation for his services during the riots which occurred later that year in Trafalgar Square on 'Bloody Sunday'. He ran a hosier's business in Wandsworth High Street and was also rate collector for Streatham. He played a full and active role in local affairs and was sadly missed when he died in 1936 aged eighty-seven.

Elmbourne Road, c. 1914. A cyclist pedals along Elmbourne Road admiring the view across Tooting Bec Common. The road is named after the 'Elmbourne', a small stream that used to flow alongside the common. Sir Harry Seeley, Conservative MP for South Battersea between 1931 and 1945, whose firm built more that 2,500 houses in the area, lived here until his death in 1960 aged eighty-eight. Other former residents include Mr A. G. White, the secretary of the Crystal Palace choir, who lived at No. 29; Ken Gordon, 'ace' cameraman with *Pathé News* in the Second World War; and Marie Hargreaves, pioneer woman journalist, who died here in 1934.

Emmanuel Road, Tooting Bec Common, c. 1911. The railway bridge opposite Cavendish Road can be seen in these photographs. The bridge was built so that residents in Streatham Hill and Balham, to the north of the railway, could gain access to Tooting Bec Common and cross the track without having to walk a long distance down the line. Considerable concern was expressed by local people when the railway sliced through the common and the bridge was a concession to this feeling. The roadway under the bridge was never pushed through to Bedford Hill as originally planned.

Emmanuel Road. The photograph above shows the junction with Rastell Avenue in around 1907, while below shows the entrance to Radbourne Road on the right as it was in around 1926. The road takes its name from the landowner, Emmanuel College, Cambridge, which purchased Hyde Farm in 1629 (see p. 102). The old farmhouse used to stand on land now occupied by Nos 46–56 Emmanuel Road. Among former residents of this road was Mr A. Josland Lobb, whose father introduced Josiah Henson, the original 'Uncle Tom' in the famous novel *Uncle Tom's Cabin*, to Queen Victoria at Windsor Castle in 1877.

The Cosy Corner, 73 Emmanuel Road, *c.* 1913. The Cosy Corner confectioners and tobacconists was run by Mrs F.A. Cowell. Two of her young assistants pose coyly, while children on the left keenly wait for the photograph to be taken so that they can spend their pennies on the magnificent display of bottled sweets that fill the windows. They are obviously far too young to be buying Player's Navy Cut or Will's Gold Flake as advertised on the windows. The shop also acted as a receiving office for Finch's Hygienic Laundries and as a telephone call office.

Elmfield Road, *c.* 1912. The turning into Cheriton Square is on the right, and in the corner house, No. 51, lived J.F. Ernest Benedict, a civil engineer. Also living here was George Waters, Senior Inspector of Custodians and Officers at the House of Lords, who was awarded the British Empire Medal in 1956 in recognition of his work at the Palace of Westminster. Balham swimming baths was built in this road in 1915 at a cost of around £12,000. Sixty-five years later the baths were completely refurbished at a cost of £1 1⁄2 million and it is known as the Balham Leisure Centre.

Endlesham Road, *c.* 1912. This road was laid out in 1868 and originally comprised some fourteen groups of villas and terraces. Among its former residents are James Henry Young, a well-known Victorian lecturer on astronomy, who lived at No. 4; Almaric Ramsey, assistant solicitor to Customs and Excise from 1868 to 1875 and professor of Indian Jurisprudence at King's College, London, between 1879 and 1899, who died at No. 105 in April 1899; Arthur Douglas Brown, who became minister of the Ramsden Road Baptist church in 1907, who lived at No. 45; and James Barber, surveyor for Streatham parish and the Wandsworth Board of Works.

Fieldhouse Road, *c.* 1920. Originally this street was known as Nonesuch Road and it is not surprising that this rather nondescript name was changed in 1901, as not many people would have wanted to live in a road whose title implied it did not exist! A more apt name was therefore chosen as the junction of this road with Emmanuel Road marks the site of Hyde Farm buildings (see p. 102) and hence the new road name Fieldhouse—indicating the site of the field adjacent to the farmhouse.

Fontenoy Road, c. 1912. The first houses were built in this road in the late 1870s and their closeness to Tooting Bec Common made this a popular road in which to live. The large homes that were built here were able to command high rents and property was available at a yearly cost, ranging from £70 to £200—the latter sum a considerable amount of money in the 1880s. Some of the houses in this street were damaged by a flying bomb which fell here in 1944.

Gaskarth Road, c. 1912. Formerly partly called Westlands Road, the name was changed by the London County Council in June 1903. An old stack pipe, with the initials LCC, stood for many years near No. 111. The road dates from the 1880s, although houses were still being erected here shortly before the First World War. The peace of the road was badly shaken in 1944 when a flying bomb fell there.

Glenfield Road, c. 1912. A horse-drawn wagon from the Balham Brewery Stores, wine merchants, plies its trade in an almost deserted Glenfield Road, while in the distance two small children near Burnbury Road look on. The street was originally known as Stackfield Road but the present name was adopted in 1898.

Balham Grove, c. 1907. Holdron's removal contracting depot is on the left, and next to it, hidden from view, is the Primitive Methodist Chapel, with a notice advising that the preacher for next Sunday's 11 a.m. service will be the Revd H. Fleming. In March 1893 Thomas Henry Higgie, member of the Adelphi Theatre Company, stage manager of Prince's theatre and Astley's amphitheatre, playwright and one of the best light comedians of his day, died at his home at No. 5 Balham Grove.

Weir Hospital, Grove Road. Formerly known as Grove Road, the street was later renamed Weir Road in honour of Benjamin Weir whose will left a generous bequest, valued at some £100,000, for the founding of a hospital for the benefit of the inhabitants of the parish of Streatham and neighbourhood. Following his death in 1902, considerable litigation was needed in order to implement Mr Weir's wishes in a manner that met the approval of the Charity Commissioners. Eventually, Weir's residence, the Hawthorns, was demolished and the hospital shown above was built on the site. This was known as the Red Cross Hospital, the Wandsworth War Memorial Maternity Home, or the Weir Hospital. Most of the hospital buildings were demolished in 1988 and the site developed for housing. The postcard below was issued in large numbers to promote Streatham's claim for its own hospital when the Charity Commissioners were proposing an alternate scheme.

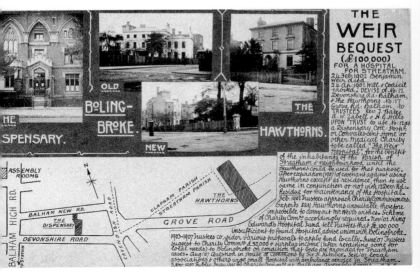

Huron Road, c. 1926. A lone car is parked in the road in an age when horse-drawn transport was still usual, as is evident from the droppings on the road. Former residents of this road include Harry Bentham, elected President of the Society of Engineers in 1938, and involved in the construction of the Blackwall Tunnel and the Surrey Commercial Docks; and Sir Arthur Johns, director of naval construction, who helped design the King Edward VII class of battleships as well as early airships and submarines. He sat on the board of inquiry into the R33 airship disaster in 1921.

Hazelbourne Road, c. 1910. This street was laid out in 1878 and like Gaskarth Road was originally partly known as Westlands Road. Hazelbourne was the name of a large house facing Balham High Road, which was demolished to make way for the building of the road. The borough boundary between Wandsworth and Lambeth passes down the centre of this road and it received widespread publicity in 1990 when it was frequently used to emphasize the difference in services, and poll and council tax rates between the two boroughs.

Haverhill Road, looking down towards Hydethorpe Road in the distance, *c.* 1912. This road was laid out in 1898 and house building began in the closing years of Queen Victoria's reign. An underground air-raid shelter was constructed on Tooting Bec Common at the opposite end of this road, which was subsequently destroyed in an enemy air raid during the Second World War.

Hillbury Road, *c.* 1910. A horse-drawn cart pauses in Hillbury Road to make a delivery to one of the large houses built here in the 1890s. Alfred Coleman (1828–1902) lived at Midhurst, 8 Hillbury Road, between 1896 and 1902. An eminent Victorian dentist, he was a surgeon and lecturer at St Bartholomew's Hospital and at the London Dental Hospital School. In 1879 he was elected President of the Odontological Society.

Honeybrook Road, *c.* 1912. A local trader, resplendent in his bowler hat and with a leather money-bag slung across his shoulder, stands proudly alongside his humble delivery cart in Honeybrook Road. Meanwhile, on the other side of the road, his young assistant stands similarly dressed, only wearing a cloth cap more befitting his status. Further down the road a window-cleaner's handcart with ladder is parked by the gas lamp-post.

Gosberton Road, *c.* 1906. Most of the houses in this street had only been built for about eight years when this photograph was taken. On the left is a small dairy handcart belonging to Curtis Dairies of 184 Balham High Road. Curtis built up his operations from his family farm in Valley Road, Streatham, where he later established one of the most advanced dairies in the country. His business was later merged to become part of United Dairies, and subsequently Unigate, which still operates from the site today.

Malwood Road, leading towards Balham Hill, *c.* 1912. This road was laid out in the mid-1870s and named in 1876. Halfway down the road a horse-drawn furniture van from R.G. Maney, art furnishers of Clapham High Road, is making a delivery. Out of view is the Church of the Ascension, built here in 1883 and consecrated the following year on 22 May. It was designed by local architect Arthur Cawston. A cast-iron Clapham parish boundary post can still be seen, bearing the inscription 'Clapham Parish 1882, Z.D. Berry & Son, Westminster'.

Mayford Road, *c.* 1926. This road dates from the mid-1890s and was developed to provide typically late Victorian terraced houses for the growing, affluent, middle classes. Mrs Ellen Mary Askham, headmistress of Winstanley Road Girls' School in Battersea, died in her home here on Christmas Day 1935. She was a much respected educationalist. She and her husband were keen supporters of the Toc H movement and regularly visited patients in St James's Hospital, where they were known as Mr and Mrs Toc H. The Toc H movement, named after Gilbert Talbot who died at Hooge on 30 July 1915, was a Christian organization of service and fellowship.

Nevis Road, *c.* 1912. This road dates from 1890 and was part of the extensive development of terraced housing which was erected between Boundaries and Marius Roads. S.C. Sanderson lived at No. 17. As a young boy he was one of the choristers of the Chapel Royal, St James's, between 1902 and 1906. He was commissioned as a lieutenant in the London Regiment in 1915 and was killed in action in France at the tragically early age of twenty-five. His commanding officer wrote of him: 'He died nobly and fearlessly holding his part of the line. In him we lose a cheery, dear friend, comrade, and a gallant officer.'

Nightingale Lane, *c.* 1909. Formerly known as Balham Wood Lane or Balham Lane, this road is one of the old routes linking Wandsworth and Clapham commons. This picture is evocative of Edwardian London, with the organ-grinder passing the time of day with a young mother, while her elder daughter chats to her baby sister in the pram. The road is said to get its name from the nightingales that sang in the trees lining the lane before it was built over.

Home for Aged Poor, *c.* 1912. The building survives today as Nightingale House, a nursing/residential complex called The Home for Aged Jews. It accommodates some four hundred residents, a number of whom have celebrated their centenary here. Rebecca Cohen marked her 101st birthday in June 1986 with a party for seventy friends and relatives. The main building was erected in 1871 to the designs of R. Richardson. It was extended in 1904 and subsequent additions have been made, including the opening of Birchlands, a unit accommodating fifty-seven residents, by Prince Philip in November 1983.

The Nightingale public house, *c.* 1910. This twin-gabled building, with the flagpole and the horse-cart outside, was built on the Old Park Estate, which was subdivided for development in 1869. To ensure the quality of buildings erected on the estate, a stipulation was included in the deeds prohibiting the construction of buildings worth less than £800, a considerable amount of money in the mid-nineteenth century.

Nightingale Lane, c. 1910. The photograph above shows the parade of shops between Western Lane and Endlesham Road. This is typical of the encroaching commercialization of the main routeways in the neighbourhood, where rows of large terraced shops, with accommodation above, were built to cater for the shopping needs of the population in the rapidly expanding suburban side-streets. The photograph below shows Glenbrook, typical of the large houses which were built along Nightingale Lane in the mid-nineteenth century. Many of these only stood for fifty years or less before they were demolished to make way for terraces of shops like that shown above.

Church of the Holy Ghost, c. 1906. A milkman, in his familiar blue-striped apron, pauses to smoke his pipe in Nightingale Square. Behind him is the Roman Catholic Church of the Holy Ghost, built in 1897 to the designs of local architect Leonard Stokes, who lived by Tooting Bec Common. The church originally accommodated three hundred worshippers, although it has subsequently been extended. A convent had been established here ten years earlier by the nuns of the Perpetual Adoration. In 1896 land was donated for the church and the foundation stone was laid that summer by the Rt. Revd Francis Bourne, Bishop of Southwark, who later became Cardinal Archbishop of Westminster. Nightingale Square dates from 1889.

Oldridge Road School, c. 1908. The London School Board opened this school on 19 June 1882, with enrolment commencing a week later. The school provided accommodation for 804 pupils: 240 boys, 240 girls, and 324 infants. The building covered an area of 26,000 sq feet and cost almost £11,000 to build, including £2,234 for the cost of the site. Within a week of opening 310 pupils had been enrolled for lessons, rising to 800 a year later (see p. 123).

Pentney Road, *c.* 1912. A young lady dressed in her finery, complete with broad-brimmed hat covered in flowers, pauses at the top of the road during a summer stroll with her young baby. The road was laid out in 1898 as part of the late Victorian development of the old Hyde Farm Estate.

Ormeley Road, *c.* 1906. A fire escape is parked at the junction with Laitwood Road on the right. This large-wheeled ladder was a permanent feature here. The fire brigade and local authorities would place such equipment at strategic locations so that it could be transported quickly to any site in the neighbourhood where an emergency occurred. Meanwhile the fire engine would make its way to the scene from the fire station and often arrived after the fire escape had turned up to help rescue people from the burning building.

Ramsden Road, c. 1920. This view from Balham High Road shows the buildings on the right of Ramsden Road, which have subsequently been demolished. Where once people visited Daniel's for ribbons and bows, they now patronize the Halifax Building Society for mortgages and loans. Balham Baptist Chapel, built in 1873 on land donated by Thomas Olney, is on the left. It was seriously damaged on 23 August 1949 when an electrical fault caused a disastrous fire in the building. It was to be five years before the church was rebuilt; it was finally reopened for services on 4 December 1954.

St Luke's Church, c. 1912. This red-brick church was built between 1883 and 1889 to the design of F.W. Hunt. The tall square bell tower was added in 1892. This bell tower, with its green copper roof complete with golden cross, has been a prominent landmark in Ramsden Road for over one hundred years. The church contains a memorial plaque to John Erskine Clarke (1827–1920), who was Chaplain in Ordinary to Queen Victoria, King Edward VII and King George V; Hon. Canon of Winchester 1875–1905 and of Southwark 1905–20; vicar of Battersea 1872–1909; and the founder and first vicar of St Luke's.

Balham Public Library, c. 1908. These photographs show the old Balham Public Library ten years after it was opened on 3 June 1898. It was designed by Sidney R.J. Smith, and its bow window and small cupola give the building a pleasing appearance. The land on which it was built was donated by Sir Henry Tate, of Tate and Lyle sugar fame. He lived at Park Hill, a large mansion at the top of Streatham Common, now occupied by St Michael's Convent. The photograph below shows both wearers of bowler hats and cloth caps enjoying some of the 130 newspapers and magazines which were stocked by the library at the turn of the century. The library was extensively renovated and enlarged in 1988/89 and was reopened to readers on 12 January 1990.

Ritherdon Road, c. 1911. This road is named after Ritherdon Brook, a local name given in the nineteenth century to the York Ditch, a small stream that flowed along what is now Dr Johnson Avenue and on through the Bedford Hill Housing Estate. This ditch was an ancient watercourse and divided the parishes of Streatham and Tooting Graveney, and separated Tooting Bec and Tooting Graveney commons. Ritherdon Road was the first road on the Heaver Estate to be developed, with houses being built there from 1890 onwards.

Rossiter Road, c. 1912. This road was laid out in the early 1860s, with houses being constructed there by James Wright from 1876 onwards. Harry Beckenham was born there in 1891, and as a boy attended Oldridge Road School (see p. 119). He was secretary to Winston Churchill at the outbreak of the First World War, and later went on to become the secretary of the British Empire Exhibition held at Wembley. He was also a director of Beckenham Brothers Ltd, which operated a motor-hire service from premises in Larch Road, Balham.

Rowfant Road, c. 1926. Houses in this road date from 1890 and the various styles of terrace show the different phases of development. Rowfant Road marks one of the ancient boundaries of Balham, which in 1548 comprised some 130 acres known as Great Balams. Today this area is bounded by Balham High Road, Nightingale Lane and Rowfant and Mayford Roads.

Corner of Tantallon Road and Mayford Road, c. 1910. Tantallon Road was originally called Tantillon Road but the 'i' was substituted for an 'a' at the turn of the twentieth century. The photograph shows the wine and spirit stores at 62 Tantallon Road, which was run for many years by Charles Albert Smallbone. He also had outlets in Tooting and at Shortlands. The delivery boy stands in the street, ready to mount his bike and rush much needed refreshment to thirsty residents.

Nine

Dan Leno

Dan Leno. Born in a slum house in St Pancras on 20 December 1860, George Galvin rose from his humble beginnings to become one of the most famous and best-loved music-hall and pantomime artists of his time. Under his stage name of Dan Leno he was billed as 'the funniest man on earth' and was the highest paid entertainer in the world, earning £20,000 a year in the 1890s. At the height of his fame he resided in South London, living at 345 Clapham Road from 1894 to 1897, during which time he became godfather to a child of the then proprietor of the Bedford Hotel, a few doors down the road. In 1898 he moved to 56 Akerman Road, Brixton, before moving eighteen months later to Springfield House in Atkins Road, Clapham Park, where he died on 31 October 1904 of a brain tumour, although exhaustion and excessive drinking had also taken their toll.

Dan Leno's funeral procession, 8 November 1904, passing along Balham High Road, with the dome of the Balham Hippodrome silhouetted on the skyline. Thousands packed the streets in sorrow to pay their last respects to the man who had made them laugh. His funeral procession was on a royal scale, taking four hours to pass the mourners lining the 3-mile route from his home in Atkins Road to the Church of the Ascension at Balham Hill, where the funeral service was held, and then to Tooting Cemetery in Blackshaw Road, for the interment. A fitting tribute for the 'King's jester and the King of jesters'.

...ooting Cemetery. The black-plumed horses of the funeral cortège stand outside the chapel at ...ooting Cemetery, their carriages laden with floral tributes, some of which are shown below. Dan ...eno's memorial, a white marble cross wreathed with ivy, stands not far from the main gates of ...ooting Cemetery in Blackshaw Road. The inscription on the base reads: 'In loving memory of ...y dear husband George Galvin "Dan Leno" who fell asleep Oct 31st 1904 aged 43 years. Here ...eeps the King of Laughter Makers. Sleep well dear heart until the King of Glory awakens thee.'

Dan Leno as Widow Twankey. 'One touch of Leno makes the whole world grin.'